Beyond the Frontier

The Story of the Trails West

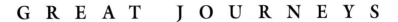

G R E A T   J O U R N E Y S

Beyond the Frontier

The Story of the Trails West

by Edward F. Dolan

BENCHMARK **B**OOKS

MARSHALL CAVENDISH
NEW YORK

With special thanks to Robert D. Johnston,
Department of History, Yale University,
for his careful reading of this manuscript.

Benchmark Books
Marshall Cavendish Corporation
99 White Plains Road
Tarrytown, NY 10591-9001

Cover photo: Denver Public Library, Western History Department
Photo research by Candlepants Incorporated
The photographs in this book are used by permission and through the courtesy of:
Missouri Historical Society: 2–3, 82. *Corbis-Bettmann*: 8, 14, 17 (top), 28, 34, 43, 46,
50–51, 52, 54, 61, 63, 66, 69, 71, 73, 76, 98, 102. *Utah State Historical Society*: 10. *Scotts
Bluff National Monument*: 13, 92, 95. *University of Wyoming American Heritage Center*: 17
(bottom). *The Bancroft Library*: 19, 78. *Kansas State Historical Society, Topeka, Kansas*: 22,
37, 44. *Denver Public Library, Western History Department*: 25, 30, 33. *The National
Archives*: 27, 85, 101. *The Butler Institute of American Art, Youngstown, Ohio*: 40. *State
Historical Society of Wisconsin*: 45. *Whitman Mission National Historic Site*: 48 (left & right).
Baldwin H. Ward/Corbis-Bettmann: 56. *San Francisco Maritime National Historic Park*:
80–81. *New York Historical Society*: 87. *UPI/Corbis-Bettmann*: 105.

Library of Congress Cataloging-in-Publication Data
Dolan, Edward F., date
Beyond the Frontier : the story of the trails West / by Edward F. Dolan.
p.   cm. — (Great journeys)
Includes bibliographical references (p.) and index.
Summary: Describes the journeys west made by many settlers in the mid-1800s—
mostly overland, but also by sea—discussing their reasons for going, the difficulties
they faced, and life on the way.
ISBN 0-7614-0969-6 (lib. bdg.)
1. West (U.S.)—History—1848–1860—Juvenile literature. 2. Overland journeys to the
Pacific—Juvenile literature. 3. Trails—West (U.S.)—History—19th century—Juvenile
literature. 4. Frontier and pioneer life—West (U.S.)—Juvenile literature. [1. Overland
journeys to the Pacific. 2. Frontier and pioneer life—West (U.S.) 3. Trails—West
(U.S.)—History. 4. West (U.S.)—History.] I. Title. II. Series: Great journeys
(Benchmark Books (Firm))
F593.D64   2000   978'.02—dc21   98-43838   CIP
AC

Contents

Also by Edward F. Dolan

Foreword

By the 1820s, the people of the United States had settled their nation from the Atlantic coast out to the Mississippi River and were pushing on to the Missouri River. Beyond the Missouri lay vast and varied lands—rolling plains, towering mountains, thick forests, and scorching deserts—that stretched for some two thousand miles to the Pacific Ocean. They were Indian lands that had been visited by a mere handful of outsiders—mostly hunters, trappers, and traders.

But things changed in the following years. In the early 1840s, a great American migration began into what newspapers called the Far West. This movement continued throughout the century, but it reached its height in the late 1840s and the 1850s. In those years, thousands of people, all searching for a new life, ventured into the western wilderness in an unending stream of covered wagons. Later, after the Civil War, while

A wagon train on the move in the great migration that took thousands of pioneers into the American Far West. The movement began in the 1840s and continued until late in the nineteenth century.

continuing to come in wagons, they also arrived in increasing numbers aboard the trains of the nation's growing network of railroads.

The migration was a combination of triumph and tragedy. While thousands made their way successfully west, thousands of others lost their lives on the trail. Thousands found new and full lives, yet thousands of others endured hardship and poverty as they carved homes out of the wilderness. And countless others—the men, women, and children of the Indian tribes that had occupied the western lands for untold generations—lost both their lives and their lands. But this migration, both triumphant and tragic, changed forever the face of America, brought about the settlement of regions that would become the nation's western, northwestern, and southwestern states, and paved the way for the millions of Americans who live there today.

South Pass provided the pioneers with an opening in the Rocky Mountains. So many wagon trains were on the road together that they often traveled three or more abreast. Painting by William Henry Jackson.

One

They Went West

When God made man,
He seemed to think it best
To make him in the East
And let him travel west.

IN THIS SHORT VERSE, A PIONEER WOMAN LEFT US HER VIEW OF WHY SO many Americans left their homes east of the Mississippi River in the 1840s and 1850s and flooded into the Far West. And flood they did. No one knows exactly how many people came west during those years when the great westward migration was in full swing, but they certainly totaled at least half a million. Some traveled by ship to the Pacific coast, but most hiked overland alongside covered wagons to their new homes.

While no complete count of the emigrants was ever made, we can get some idea of their number from a few records that have been left to us. One tally was made of the pioneers as they pushed through a gap in the Rocky Mountains called South Pass, a gently rising path that enabled the covered wagons to get across the towering mountains. South Pass was used by some 350,000 travelers between 1840 and 1869.

Two other tallies followed the 1848 discovery of gold in California. When the news of the find reached the outside world, farmers dropped their plows, office workers fled their desks, and shopkeepers closed their stores. They all headed west, dizzy with the dream of quick riches. More than 25,000 hopefuls rushed overland in 1849 alone and were soon joined by thousands more. In addition, some 100,000 arrived by ship in the next few years.

Still more tallies: Two major forts on the overland route—Kearny and Laramie—kept logs of the travelers who trudged past their gates. At Kearny, some 24,000 adults—20,000 men and 4,000 women—were counted between 1849 and mid-1853 (the report did not say whether the total included children). Fort Laramie, 330 miles to the west, reported seeing 6,034 emigrants on June 17, 1850, the peak day that year.

Western motion pictures have given us the impression that the wagon trains each made their way west alone, rumbling along in single file. This was true at the start of the migration, when just a few people were on the road, as was the case in 1842 when the first emigrants set out for the northwestern region known as Oregon Country. But it was far from true when thousands were on the move. There could be as many as five trains all rumbling along abreast, separated by several hundred yards or several miles. As pioneer James Wilkins wrote in his diary in June 1850:

Find a great many companies continually in sight. In fact, it is one continued stream. As far as we can see, both in front and near the horizon is dotted with white covers [the covered wagons] of emigrants, like a string of beads.

Nebraska's Fort Kearny was a major stopping point along the westward trail. The fort provided the emigrants with services that ranged from wagon repairs to advice on the road conditions ahead.

People from many walks of life joined the great migration—from honest, hardworking families to cardsharps. All were looking for new lives in the West.

Who were all these people who crowded the westbound roadways? Why did they sell their homes, quit their jobs, bid farewell to loved ones, and strike out for the unknown that lay beyond the horizon of the setting sun?

In answer to the first question, they came from all walks of life. Name any occupation you wish—from farmer, carpenter, and store clerk to lawyer, undertaker, and gambler—and it could be found in any wagon train. Look for the young and the old, the strong and the weak, and the prosperous and the poor and you would find them all.

Francis Parkman, the historian who came west in the 1840s to make his famed Indian study, wrote descriptions of the various emigrants he encountered. Often his words were harsh, as in what he said about a group that entered Fort Laramie while he was camped there:

> Tall awkward men, in brown homespun; women, with cadaverous faces and long lank figures. . . . They seemed like men totally out of their element; bewildered and amazed, like a troop of schoolboys lost in the woods. . . . For the most part, they were the rudest and most ignorant of the frontier population; they knew absolutely nothing of the country and its inhabitants; they had already experienced much misfortune.

But he treated others more kindly, describing them as intelligent and hardworking people. And he was completely charmed by one couple—a pretty girl sporting a dainty parasol as she rode beside a young man:

> The girl and her beau apparently found something very agreeable in each other's company, for they kept more than a mile in advance of their party.

Though many emigrants were poor, you would rarely see the poverty-stricken on the westbound trails. The travelers had to have money for food, tools, weapons, the covered wagon, its spare parts, and its teams. In all, a family had to be able to afford between $700 and $1500 for the trip. This was a large sum, often a family's life savings, in the mid-1800s.

Though they came from all walks of life, the emigrants shared one trait. They were restless, venturesome, curious to see what lay beyond the horizon and not afraid to go and look. This should not surprise us. They were, remember, the descendants of people who had been daring enough to leave their homes in Europe—from such diverse lands as England, Germany, Scandinavia, and Italy—and cross the Atlantic to build a new life in a wilderness.

So, in answer to the second question, it could be said that history was repeating itself. The pioneers were venturing west for the very reason their forefathers had come to America. They were looking for a fresh start.

The Mormons are a good example. Members of the Church of Jesus Christ of Latter Day Saints, they wanted a new life in which they could practice their religion free of persecution. After Joseph Smith founded the church at Fayette, New York, in 1830, he and his people had to move several times to escape the anger and prejudice of their neighbors. They tried settling in Ohio, Missouri, and Illinois, but trouble followed them, until Smith was killed by an armed mob in 1846. His chief aide, Brigham Young, took his place and led the Mormons on an epic march from Illinois to the Utah desert, where they built Salt Lake City.

The greatest single reason for coming west was to find a parcel of fertile land for farming. In the 1830s, the people living east of the Mississippi began hearing reports of the wondrous lands to be found in the Far West. The earliest stories came from fur traders, mountain men, and missionaries seeking to Christianize the Indians. These glowing accounts inspired the first pioneers to try their luck out there in the early 1840s. Then back across the Mississippi came *their* reports of its wonders. More and more people abandoned their old lives to go questing after new ones.

Who could blame them for moving? The pictures that were painted of the Far West were breathtaking. For instance, a popular booklet of the day had this to say about Oregon Country:

As far as its producing qualities are concerned, Oregon cannot be outdone, whether in wheat, oats, rye, barley, buckwheat, peas, beans, potatoes, turnips, cabbages, onions, parsnips, carrots, beets, currents, gooseberries, strawberries, apples, peaches, pears, or . . .

Seeking freedom from religious persecution, members of the Mormon faith followed their leader, Brigham Young, from Illinois to the Utah desert in 1846.

Brigham Young's followers posed for this photograph at South Pass en route to Utah, where they would build Salt Lake City.

After that word *or* came four words bound to fill a family's mind with happy visions: *fat and healthy babies.*

The promise of a healthy life in a region where the air was said to be purer was enough to make any family pull up its roots and move. Diseases had long attacked the settled lands east of the Mississippi. Typhoid fever, tuberculosis, malaria, and scarlet fever had ravaged the cities and countryside alike for decades, taking thousands of lives. Especially dreaded in the South was the specter of yellow fever. And feared everywhere was cholera, a highly infectious and often fatal disease now known to be caused by a bacterium that poisons water. A cholera epidemic erupted in Asia in the 1830s, spread to Europe, and then to the United States aboard European ships. During the following twenty years it moved inland. It even pursued the wagon trains across the plains and was, for several years, a main cause of death on the trail.

How did thousands of people make their way into the Far West? They came by a network of trails, plus two main sea routes. We're going to travel these pathways in the course of this book. The most used of their number was widely known as the overland route. It began life as the Oregon Trail, which stretched from Missouri across some two thousand miles of untamed land to the northwestern region known then as Oregon Country and now as the states of Oregon and Washington.

The Oregon Trail served as an avenue to two other major routes. At one point along the way, a branch angled off to the southwest and made its way to the Great Salt Lake in the future state of Utah. A second branch, which was located some 150 miles beyond the first, also angled off to the southwest. It climbed the Sierra Nevada Mountains and came down their western slopes to the Pacific coast. The first branch was forged by Brigham Young and his followers and was named for them—the Mormon Trail. The second branch was the California Trail.

Two sea routes also led to California. Both were widely used during the gold rush of 1849 and the early 1850s. One carried passengers from

Death from illness and accident stalked the wagon trains. Especially feared was cholera, a disease that could kill its victims in a matter of hours.

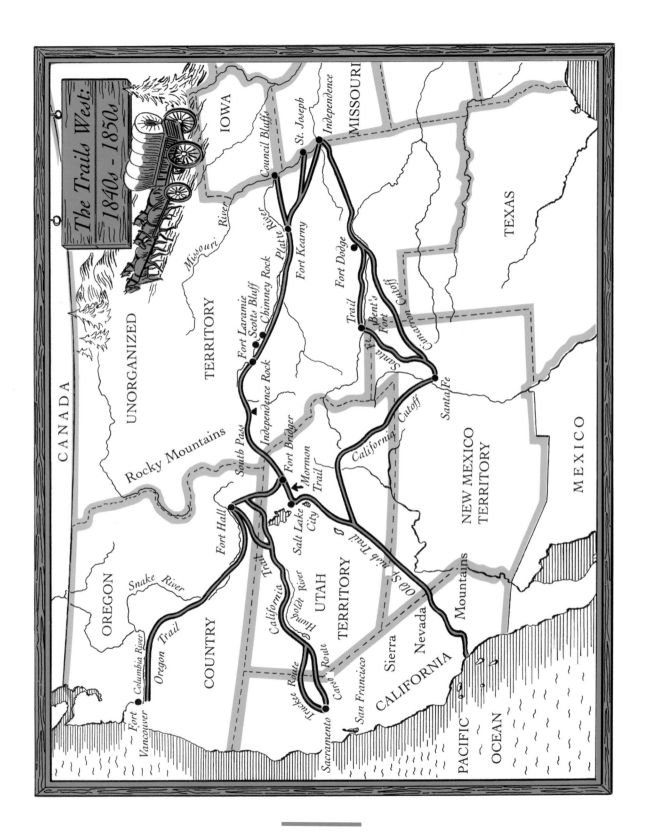

The Trails West: 1840s - 1850s

CANADA

UNORGANIZED TERRITORY

IOWA

MISSOURI

TEXAS

Missouri River

Council Bluffs

St. Joseph

Independence

Fort Laramie
Scotts Bluff
Chimney Rock

Platte River

Fort Kearny

Fort Dodge

Santa Fe Trail

Bent's Fort

Cimarron Cutoff

Rocky Mountains

South Pass

Independence Rock

Fort Bridger

Mormon Trail

Santa Fe

California Cutoff

NEW MEXICO TERRITORY

MEXICO

OREGON COUNTRY

Snake River

Fort Hall

Oregon Trail

California Trail

Salt Lake City

UTAH TERRITORY

Old Spanish Trail

Humboldt River

Carson Route

Sierra Nevada Mountains

Columbia River

Fort Vancouver

Truckee Route

San Francisco

Sacramento

CALIFORNIA

PACIFIC OCEAN

the eastern seaboard and Europe south through the Atlantic Ocean to the foot of South America and then into the Pacific for a voyage north to California's port of San Francisco.

The second route, a shortcut, took ships west across the Caribbean Sea to the east coast of Panama. The Panama Canal had yet to be built, so passengers went ashore for a trek through the jungle to the Pacific side of the isthmus. There they camped on the seashore until boarding a ship for the rest of the trip to San Francisco.

The overland route holds the distinction of being the most heavily traveled pathway. But it was not the oldest. That honor goes to a trail that reached to and then far beyond a settlement in the region that later became the state of New Mexico. This is the first roadway that we'll travel into the wilderness: the Santa Fe Trail.

The Santa Fe Trade *by famed western artist Frederic Remington. The Santa Fe Trail was one of the earliest pathways leading beyond the frontier. It was first used solely for trade and later as a roadway for settlers planning to establish farms, ranches, and businesses.*

Two

The Santa Fe Trail

FIVE HORSEMEN RODE AWAY FROM THEIR CAMP NEAR THE VILLAGE OF Franklin, Missouri, at dawn on September 1, 1821. They sat easily in the saddle as their mounts trotted toward the western horizon. Trudging after them came several mules, each weighed down by large rawhide sacks crammed with cooking utensils, blankets, beads, and colored cloths—all meant to please the Arapaho and Cheyenne tribes of the Rocky Mountains.

Leading the party was William Becknell, a red-bearded man who had long made his living by searching out salt licks (places, such as springs, containing deposits of salt that animals like to lick) in Missouri and peddling their contents to storekeepers. Now he was starting something new. He was heading into the Rockies with four companions to swap his goods for Indian horses. The animals would be in great demand by the settlers now crowding into Missouri.

Becknell was sure that his venture would prove a success. It would, but in a way he had not planned. It would win him a place in the history of the American West.

In the next weeks, Becknell led his party across Missouri. He entered the region of Kansas in October, came to the Arkansas River, moved west along its banks to Fort Dodge, and then on to the future state of Colorado. Here, he reined up at a small river called the Purgatoire that flowed across his path. And here he made a decision that took him a step closer to winning his place in history. November was bringing on winter fast. He decided not to push into the Rockies. They would soon be blanketed with snow. Instead, he would follow the Purgatoire southwest to warmer weather.

His change of plan took Becknell along the river to the Sangre de Cristo Mountains, which stretched down from Colorado to the Spanish territory of New Mexico. It was some of the roughest country he had ever seen. His men had to chop a trail through dense woods. Then, on entering a gap known as Raton Pass, they found their way blocked by piles of rocks and boulders. There was no way to get past and so, cursing, the riders swung down from their saddles and hauled the rocks and boulders over to the side to clear a path for themselves. It was a backbreaking job that took two days to complete.

They were exhausted by the time they left Raton Pass behind and rode down the mountainside to the Rock River. But on reaching its banks on November 13, they immediately forgot their fatigue. They sighted a cloud of dust in the distance. It churned toward them and turned into a troop of mounted soldiers in Mexican uniforms.

Becknell watched tensely as the riders approached. He was sure that by now he had crossed the border between the United States and Spain's New Mexico. He was on land that the Spanish had held for three centuries as part of their giant colony, Old Mexico. They had zealously kept outsiders from coming into the region to trade with its people. That

Raton Pass delayed William Becknell and his men for two days while they cleared a path through the rocks. The pass continued to slow the progress of traders until it was improved by work crews from Bent's Fort.

trade had always belonged to Spain, and Spain alone. But just a few months ago, the Mexicans had rebelled against their Spanish masters and had overthrown them.

Becknell now wondered if the Mexicans would be any different from the Spanish in their dealings with outsiders. Would they angrily order him back to the United States? Would they jail him as the Spanish had jailed a few of the trappers and hunters who had ventured across the border? Or would they rob him of his wares?

He got his answer as soon as the troop reined to a halt. The young lieutenant in charge cantered up to him and extended a welcoming hand. With the end of Spanish rule, the lieutenant said, things were to be different in New Mexico, much friendlier than ever in the past.

All the while that the Spanish had ruled the area, they had brought in trade goods from the outside world via two routes. One had come overland all the way from Mexico City. The other had brought ships from Europe to the city of Vera Cruz on the eastern coast of Old Mexico, where their cargoes were then sent by caravan some 1,500 miles to the towns and settlements of New Mexico, among them its small capital city, Santa Fe.

But now, with the Spanish gone, the trade from Mexico City and Vera Cruz had dwindled to nothing. The people of New Mexico were hungry for both the necessities and luxuries of life. Consequently, the lieutenant explained, traders from the outside world were welcome.

Becknell explained that he had traveled some seven hundred miles from Missouri and was passing through to the Indian tribes farther on. Smiling, the lieutenant shook his head and urged the trader to stay in New Mexico and go no farther than Santa Fe, just three days away. He promised Becknell that he would sell his merchandise there at a fine profit.

Becknell mulled over that promise. He did not know if the Mexican was telling the truth or sending him into a trap that would see him robbed of his wares. But he was a trader. He had to take risks if he hoped for a profit. All right. Santa Fe it would be.

It was another fateful decision on Becknell's part, and it brought him and his men into Santa Fe three days later. The town immediately struck them as a sorry-looking place. It had narrow, dirt streets that were lined with one-story houses made of a material the traders had never seen—the

The village of Santa Fe, New Mexico. Becknell's men found it a dirty place, but no dirtier than other towns along the frontier.

Though not impressed with the look of Santa Fe, Becknell was taken with its people. They were friendly and eager to purchase his goods.

sun-dried mud called adobe. In 1807, U.S. Army lieutenant Zebulon Pike had been detained by Spanish troops while exploring New Mexico and had been brought into Santa Fe. He had not been at all impressed by its houses, writing in his diary that they looked like "the fleet of flat-bottom boats" that sailed the Ohio River.

Though Becknell shared Pike's view of the town, he was impressed by its 4,800 people. They lived in squalor, yes, but they had money and were ready to spend it. As soon as the traders spread their goods out on the ground, eager brown faces pressed in on all sides. Buyers and sellers began to bargain in a combination of Spanish, English, and sign language. Everything from mirrors to bolts of cloth changed hands for silver and gold coins, furs, and raw wool. The traders were soon asking for—and getting—prices that were five hundred times greater than the cost of the goods.

All the stock disappeared in a few hours. But Becknell remained for weeks in Santa Fe so that he could learn exactly what the people wanted most to buy in the future. He started home in December, with the trip finally ending on Franklin's main street on January 29, 1822.

The townspeople were astonished when he told them of his success and of how eager the New Mexicans were for more trade goods—everything from fine silks to spices to hammers, nails, and saws. Eyes widened in disbelief when he said that he and his men had earned $10,000 for their efforts. But all doubt vanished when he removed the rawhide bags of silver and gold from his pack mules. A companion cut one bag open. Coins poured from it and rattled across the stone sidewalk.

And as if the coins weren't enough proof of success, Becknell told the story of young Fanny Marshall, the sister of one of his men. She had invested sixty dollars in merchandise for the trip and was now to receive nine hundred dollars in return.

The people of Missouri had been like Becknell on the day when the Mexican lieutenant galloped up to him. They knew that the Spanish had been ousted from New Mexico but did not know if the new government would open the region to outsiders. Becknell showed that the border was indeed open and the people beyond it eager to do business with the United States. As a result, even though a few other traders were also probing into New Mexico, William Becknell became known as the man who blazed the road to Santa Fe—the Santa Fe Trail.

Traders relax for a moment on the Santa Fe Trail. Painting by William Henry Jackson.

Three

Caravans into Danger

BECKNELL BEGAN PLANNING HIS NEXT FORAY AS SOON AS HE RETURNED to Franklin. Just four months later, in May 1822, he set off again, cementing his reputation as the Father of the Santa Fe Trail.

Becknell made two changes in the way he traveled that would affect thousands of pioneers who came in his wake.

First, he decided not to use pack animals this time. Since each mule could haul only three hundred pounds of cargo, he would need too many animals to carry enough goods for his customers. Instead, he would use wagons. A good-sized wagon, one pulled by eight mules, could haul as much as three tons! It could rake in a fortune. He was right. The 1822 trip turned a profit of $100,000.

The wagons pioneered by Becknell soon became the most popular mode of transport along the trail. They were fitted with canvas covers stretched over arched wooden frames to protect their cargoes from the

31

weather. Covered wagons were eventually seen along all the westward trails. From a distance, they looked like sailing ships moving across seas of grass. They soon won the nickname prairie schooners.

Becknell's second change stemmed from his memory of the boulders of Raton Pass. Knowing that his wagons would never get past them, he checked some early maps of the area and decided to try an alternate route.

In May 1822, he led three wagons and twenty-one men to Santa Fe. The wagons carried five thousand dollars worth of merchandise. As before, he followed the Arkansas River to Fort Dodge. Then, just twenty miles later, Becknell put his new route to the test. He crossed to the south bank of the Arkansas and took the wagons through a desert to the Cimarron River at the western edge of today's state of Oklahoma. He forded the Cimarron and rolled past the southern foot of the Sangre de Cristo Mountains to Santa Fe. His new route had worked, saving him more than two hundred miles.

The route was quickly dubbed the Cimarron Cutoff and was used in place of the Raton Pass route by many traders in the next years. But it was a dangerous choice. The traders had to make their way through merciless heat and blinding dust storms, all the while risking death from thirst and attack by hostile Indians.

Becknell met the danger of thirst on his very first desert crossing. He and his party ran out of water and could find none for two days. In the broiling heat, their tongues swollen from thirst, they became delirious and saw mirages of lakes, rivers, and even wondrous cities of gold. Then, when death was staring them in the face, they managed to kill a buffalo whose stomach was filled with water. One trader later said that nothing had ever tasted finer than his first swallow of that "filthy beverage."

The earliest traders passed without fear through tribal lands, among them those of the Osage, Arapaho, and Comanche. They were simply going to and from Santa Fe and posed no threat to the tribal hunting grounds. Nor did they want to settle on them. It was widely believed that

Thirst and the threat of dehydration were ever-present on the Cimarron Cutoff. Each wagon carried its own barrel of water.

Native Americans never made war unless their land was imperiled.

They were right in thinking themselves safe, at least for a time. At first, the only conflicts arose from bands that were out not to murder them but to steal their horses and mules. An important form of Indian commerce was horse theft. The Osage were known to take the animals one day and sell them the next. The Arapaho were likewise ardent horse thieves. In 1826, a band of Arapaho warriors closed in on a camp of twelve traders alongside the Cimarron River. The outnumbered traders were not harmed but had to sit throughout the night and watch as the Arapaho drove off their entire herd of more than five hundred horses and mules.

In time, however, these relations would turn deadly. Trouble grew

An artist's rendition of a Comanche assault. The first traders faced little conflict with the Indians because the tribes thought the outsiders posed no threat to their ancient hunting grounds. But when settlers began to overrun their lands, Native Americans fought back.

when the trail speared out from Santa Fe, connecting smaller towns and settlements in need of goods from the outside world. Among them were Albuquerque in New Mexico, El Paso in Texas, and Chihuahua and Sonora in Old Mexico. Then settlers joined the traders, establishing farms and ranches. The Native Americans who lived in the region saw their lands overrun by outsiders, and they struck back. The Apache attacked south to El Paso and Chihuahua and terrified the settlers into deserting entire towns along the way. The Comanche swooped down on Texas ranches, took away horses for future sale, and grabbed prisoners for ransom. It was a bloody drama that would be played out for years in the Southwest.

Throughout the history of the trail, traders drove their wagons to

The Comanche Incident

One of the earliest deadly encounters on the westward trail occurred in 1828. Two young men became separated from their trading party when they were traveling home. They made camp and, thinking that they were in no danger, rolled themselves in their blankets and went to sleep. It was a tragic mistake. A band of Comanches crept up to the campsite, shot the two, and vanished into the dark.

The next day the trading party came upon the campsite. They found one of the young men dead and the other severely wounded. The wounded man's friends carried him forty miles along the homeward-bound trail before he died.

They were burying him beside the Cimarron River when six Comanche riders appeared on the opposite bank. They stared quietly at the traders. It is likely that the Indians knew nothing of the killing. Otherwise, they would not have come near the burial site, where they were greeted with cold stares. Sensing the anger in the Americans, they turned to ride away.

At that moment, one of the traders swung his rifle to his shoulder and fired a shot across the river. It sent a Comanche pony tumbling. The rider was killed an instant later in a hail of rifle balls. Then there was a second burst from the burial site. Only one man survived the storm of gunfire. He galloped off to his tribe with the news.

The Comanches were enraged. They chased after the traders' caravan and made off with nearly a thousand of its horses and mules. Several days later, still in a fury, they attacked a caravan that came into view, killed a man, and stole the horses and mules. The survivors had to travel by foot for more than a week, mostly at night, laden with heavy sacks of Santa Fe silver, before they found horses for the remainder of their journey.

Santa Fe and beyond just once a year because the round trip took several months to complete. They set out in the fair weather of spring, traveling in caravans that sometimes numbered more than a hundred wagons.

The first traders "jumped off" from Franklin. But when a flood washed the town away in 1828, they turned to the nearby village of Independence instead. Independence became the gateway to the Santa Fe Trail and also to all the major routes west.

To see what life was like on the trail, let's say that you are a trader bound for Santa Fe in the late 1830s. You first take your wagon out of Independence to a spot called Council Grove. Here you join the other wagons making the trip and become part of a caravan. The caravan is necessary for safety's sake. You can never tell when you'll need help because of Indian trouble or an accident.

You and your fellow traders, as well as the wagoners who drive the teams, are an independent lot. None of you likes to take orders from anyone. But you're smart enough to know that the caravan has to be organized if it is to survive the hard days ahead. And so you elect a leader, a man known for his good sense, courage, and previous experience on the trail. From now on, his word will be law. He has the right to banish anyone whose behavior puts the caravan at risk.

In the trail's first years, mules were used as wagon teams. Since then, they have been mostly replaced by oxen, animals that are easier to handle. But some mules are still used and you'll get a look at their wild natures each dawn when the caravan leader yells "Catch up! Catch up!" It is the signal for the wagoners to get their teams into harness for the day's march. They manage to yoke the docile oxen without much trouble. But the mules, bucking in anger or fright, refuse to cooperate. They dash in circles and kick up choking clouds of dust while the wagoners chase them down and wrestle them into harnesses.

In his diary, trader Josiah Gregg describes the wild time that followed the leader's call of "Catch up!" on the first morning of his 1831 trip:

Fording the Arkansas River was often dangerous. The wagon teams has to cross as fast as possible to avoid being trapped in the quicksand that coated the river bottom.

The woods and dales resound with the gleeful yells of the light-hearted wagoners, who, weary of inaction, and filled with joy at the prospect of getting away, become clamorous in the extreme. . . . Each teamster vies with his fellows who shall be soonest ready. . . . It is a matter of boastful pride to be the first to cry out, 'All's set!'

The uproarious bustle which follows, the halloing of those in pursuit of the animals, the exclamations which the unruly brutes call forth from their wrathful drivers, together with the clatter of bells, the rattle of yokes and harness, the jangle of chains, all conspire to produce a clamorous confusion.

The confusion is slowly replaced by order as the teams are harnessed. Now the leader shouts "Stretch out!" Bullwhips crackle. Harnesses groan. Wheels begin to turn. The caravan is on its way.

Next comes the shout, "Fall in!" The wagons never travel in single file; that would string them out in a long line and make them vulnerable to attack. Rather, at the command "Fall in," they move into lines of two to four wagons abreast. The caravan becomes more compact and, in the event of trouble, the lines can be quickly shifted into a hollow square that becomes a fortress for the traders.

At dusk, the wagons form the same square. The mules and oxen are tethered to picket ropes outside the square for grazing through the night.

They are herded inside at dawn for the carnival of "catch up."

On an average day, you cover between fifteen and twenty miles. At last, the Arkansas River comes into view. You follow its northern bank past Fort Dodge and reach the point where you can choose between the two routes to Santa Fe. You can ford the Arkansas and take the Cimarron Cutoff, or you can continue on to the Purgatoire River and then head through the Sangre de Cristo Mountains.

Each route has its advantages and disadvantages. If you choose the cutoff, you go dashing across the Arkansas. The river is shallow, but its bottom is coated with quicksand and speed is vital if the wagons and teams are to avoid being trapped. The oxen have no trouble, but the mules, their eyes rolling in terror, slip and fall. Some of the wagons become mired up to their wheel hubs and have to be pulled free. Then comes that desert of merciless heat and endless thirst. But once you've crossed it, you'll have saved yourself some ten or more days of travel time.

The march over the Sangre de Cristo Mountains adds long miles but holds two advantages. First, just before reaching the Purgatoire River, you come upon a giant trading post—Bent's Fort. It is built of thick adobe walls that girdle a field large enough to accept the trail's biggest caravans. The area contains workshops, stables, corrals, storehouses, offices, and living quarters for the more than one hundred workers. The post is operated by William Bent and was built in 1834. It does a brisk trade in buffalo hides and beaver pelts with the surrounding tribes and the trappers.

Here you stop to relax and, if necessary, repair your wagon. Then, as you move along the Purgatoire River, another advantage awaits you: wood and water are more plentiful than in the desert. And yet another advantage: Bent has smoothed the path through the Sangre de Cristo Mountains and has made travel somewhat easier. The route is known as the mountain branch of the Santa Fe Trail.

But in the minds of many traders, these advantages cannot outweigh the greatest plus of the Cimarron Cutoff—all the miles that are saved.

Though the mountain route is chosen by some caravans (usually the ones with smaller wagons), it will never match the popularity of the cutoff.

No matter your route, there comes at last the finest moment of the journey: when you catch sight of Santa Fe. The men in your caravan are like all the others that have come here before you. There are yells of jubilation. Hats fly into the air. There is the sudden roar of gunfire.

In some caravans, the long-standing order of march is forgotten. The men break ranks and send their wagons thundering toward town in their eagerness to be done with the trail. In others, there is no wild dash. The traders and wagoners know that as they make their way into Santa Fe, they'll be closely watched by its people. They spend their time "rubbing up" so that they will be bathed, shaven, and dressed in their best clothing on driving proudly into town.

And so, either dashing into Santa Fe aboard a speeding wagon or arriving sedately in your best finery, you begin a visit that may last for several weeks. But this being the 1830s, you may remain only a few days before moving on to do business in Albuquerque, El Paso, and perhaps even Chihuahua in Old Mexico.

If you continue to trade along the trail, you will see it change. An increasing number of people will come as settlers, looking farther and farther west. Santa Fe will become the starting point for families bound for the fertile reaches of southern California. They will follow an arcing trail with two names to the Pacific coast. First, they will move northwest along what is called the California Cutoff and enter Utah. There, the roadway becomes the Spanish Trail, which will drop them southwest to the city of Los Angeles. Southern California can also be reached by following the Gila River along the border with Old Mexico.

Though you and many Americans have traveled the Santa Fe Trail, you will hear tales of yet another route west. It lies to the north, tracing a rugged path west from Missouri and then northwest to the Pacific coast. It's called the Oregon Trail.

The Oregon Trail *by Albert Bierstadt, the first major artist to put the wonders of America's Far West on canvas.*

Four

The Oregon Trail

THE OREGON TRAIL, LIKE THE SANTA FE TRAIL, WAS FORGED BY RUGGED traders who pressed deep into the western wilds in the early 1800s. Their quest took them through the Rocky Mountains and out to what was called Oregon Country in the Pacific Northwest.

They went there for just one thing—beaver pelts. These pelts were the basis for a giant industry, the manufacture and sale of men's hats. At the time, countless American and European men saw the beaver hat as the finest headwear that money could buy. It was so popular that manufacturers happily paid ten dollars each for skins that the traders bought from the Indians for a dollar.

Among the adventurers who forged the Oregon Trail was William Hunt. While working for New York fur dealer John Jacob Astor, Hunt tramped overland from Missouri to Oregon Country between 1810 and 1812. On his arrival, he helped to found the fur trading post that, named in honor of his employer, became today's city of Astoria. For much of his journey, Hunt marched through unexplored territory. His final miles stretched along a route almost identical to the path later etched by the trail.

Other traders soon came in his wake, all searching for beaver in lands through which the trail would someday run. In 1812, Robert Stuart stumbled upon a wide gap in the Rockies. The gently rising grass-covered avenue of dry grass called South Pass would give the emigrant wagons a passage through the towering mountains.

Some twenty years later, in 1834, Nathaniel Jarvis Wyeth founded Idaho's first settlement, the trading post known as Fort Hall in the south-eastern section of the future state. Then, in 1843, the West's most famous trapper and scout, Jim "Old Gabe" Bridger, nailed up his own trading post, a mud-spattered cabin just over the border in Wyoming, which he named Fort Bridger. Both posts became major rest and supply stops for pioneers traveling the Oregon Trail.

By the mid-1830s, the trail was well established. On leaving Independence, it merged for some miles with the Santa Fe Trail before swinging away to the northwest. After following the Platte River for miles, it then rose through South Pass, ran by Forts Bridger and Hall, and entered Oregon Country. Finally, after traversing the Blue Mountains and the Cascades, it came to an end at Fort Vancouver on the Columbia River, some two thousand miles from its start.

Oregon Country itself was a vast area that began at the southern border of today's state of Oregon and extended north through present-day Washington and Canada's British Columbia to the southern border of Alaska, a region occupied at the time by the Russians. For some time, four nations—Russia, Spain, Great Britain, and the United States—claimed a right to the area. Russia and Spain gave up their holdings in the early 1800s, with Russia continuing to remain in Alaska.

Britain and the United States, according to an 1818 treaty, shared

The quest for pelts that were made into the vastly popular beaver hat brought the first trappers and traders west along the Oregon Trail.

Mountain man and trader—Jim "Old Gabe" Bridger

Jim Bridger's fort and trading post in Wyoming. Built in 1843, it quickly became a major stopping place for the westward-bound emigrants. Drawing by James F. Wilkins.

Oregon Country until trouble between the two caused them to divide it into two separate regions in 1848. An agreement placed the area's southern reaches (Oregon and Washington) in American hands and renamed them Oregon Territory. The northern sector (British Columbia) went to Great Britain.

In the early 1800s fur traders and Native Americans made up the bulk of Oregon's population. Until the late 1820s, no one paid much attention to the region's fine soil or its potential for farming. No one, that is, aside from a young Boston schoolteacher and minister named Hall Jackson Kelley. After hearing a U.S. congressman speak of Oregon's

natural wonders, he became obsessed with the idea of leading three thousand New Englanders there to farm and plant "the vine of Christianity and the germ of Civil Freedom." In 1832, with this aim in mind, he formed the American Society for Encouraging the Settlement of the Oregon Territory. He attracted five hundred members to the society and told them that Oregon could become "the loveliest and most envied country on earth" once they had settled and tamed it. But his descriptions of its magnificent farmlands aching to be planted, its mountains, its forests, and its teeming animal life went for naught. He never drew enough people for his planned trek west.

Kelley, however, did manage to travel to Oregon on his own—only to be frustrated by an unlucky turn of events. Boarding a ship in 1833, he sailed across the Caribbean to the east coast of Mexico. He then hiked overland to the Pacific coast and ventured north to California. There, needing money, he took a job with some traders who were driving horses and mules to Fort Vancouver. They were joined along the way by several men, who lent a hand herding the animals. When the party arrived in Vancouver, residents recognized the men who had recently joined them as horse thieves. Since Kelley and the traders were traveling with them, they too were branded as thieves. Kelley eventually convinced the Vancouver officials of his innocence and returned to New England. But his Oregon dream was at an end.

Though his life's ambition was never realized, Kelley played a major role in the early settlement of Oregon. All that he had to say about the region in his writings and public speeches helped to inspire the first of a growing number of people to abandon their midwestern and eastern homes.

Among the earliest settlers were Presbyterian ministers Marcus

Oregon's early fur trappers and traders had little interest in raising crops. The desire to farm came later, bringing a flood of settlers to the region in the 1840s.

Narcissa and Marcus Whitman

Whitman and Henry Spalding. With their wives, Narcissa Whitman and Eliza Spalding, they set out along the Oregon Trail in 1836. The four-some did not travel in a wagon train (these were yet to come) but rattled along in the wake of a large band of French and American fur traders.

Narcissa and Eliza became the first white women to cross the Rockies and enter Oregon Country. Narcissa was a high-spirited woman who, in her letters home, left a fascinating record of her life on the trail. She reveled in all that she experienced along the way: the Indian women who crowded around her to shake her hand at one stop, the joy she felt when washing her clothes for the first time in weeks, the western hills that reminded her of her New York home, and a magnificent sunset viewed from a mountain at five thousand feet. All of her experiences, from the simplest to the most challenging, went into her letters. She even wrote of what it was like to eat on the trail:

Our table is the ground, our table cloth is an India rubber cloth, used when it rains as a cloak; our dishes are made of tin—basins for tea cups, iron spoons and plates for each of us, and several pans for milk and to put our meat in when we wish to set it on the table—and each one carries his own knife. . . . It is the fashion of all this country to imitate the Turks. We take a blanket and lay down by the table.

But there were moments when the rigors of the journey, the endless miles, the periodic lack of food and water, taxed her spirit to the breaking point. One day, when the trip seemed without end, she wrote: "Have six weeks steady journeying before us. Will the Lord give me patience to endure it? Long for rest but must not murmur."

She and her companions survived those six weeks, and more. Finally the weary travelers arrived at their destination. The Whitmans established a mission for the Cayuse Indians near Walla Walla in present-day Washington. The Spaldings built their mission to the east for the Nez Percé. Both couples worked among the Indians for years, with the Whitman mission also serving as a rest stop for emigrants who, after besting the Oregon Trail, were looking for the acres on which to settle.

Because of the speeches of Hall Jackson Kelley and the letters and reports sent home by Narcissa Whitman and other early pioneers, a number of adventurous families decided to gamble their futures on the promise of a fine new life in Oregon. At first, their numbers were few. Thirteen set out in 1840. The first wagon train was organized a year later and departed Independence with seventy pioneers.

In 1842 and 1843, the traffic to Oregon Country grew at a healthy

Death for the Whitmans

The Whitmans labored at their mission for more than a decade. For much of that time, the Cayuse, who had seen almost no white people before, looked on Narcissa as a goddess and Marcus as a powerful medicine man. But in 1847, these peaceful relations were severed.

First, Marcus Whitman, intent on keeping the Cayuse from stealing the mission's crop of melons, injected the ripening fruit with a strong cathartic. When several people fell seriously ill after eating the melons, his strategy did nothing but anger the Indians. Next, a group of emigrants triggered an epidemic of measles among the Cayuse. The Whitmans were powerless to save the lives of many of the afflicted Indian children. Unlike the white children, they had not built up an immunity to help them survive the disease.

The tribe was convinced that the deaths of their children were part of a plot. On November 29, the enraged Indians, certain that Marcus was trying to get rid of their tribe and take over their lands, attacked the mission. They burned its buildings to the ground and killed Narcissa and Marcus, along with seven other whites. Fifty-one women and children were taken into captivity.

The attack led to a war that saw the Cayuse tribe almost completely wiped out.

rate: 125 pioneers in 1842, followed by 875 in 1843. But that growth paled when compared to what followed. In 1844, the number jumped to 1,475, and it reached 2,500 in 1845. Why? Because the nation was suddenly caught in what the press called Oregon Fever. The condition was triggered in part by Oregon's growing reputation as a magnificent land for settlement and in part by a vision that had taken shape in recent years throughout the United States—the vision of Manifest Destiny.

Manifest Destiny was the belief that America was duty-bound to extend its borders from sea to sea, from the Atlantic all the way to the Pacific, and from Canada down to Old Mexico. The United States and

The mission established by Narcissa Whitman and her husband near present-day Walla Walla, Washington

A Currier and Ives lithograph of a pioneer home in the Far West presents an idealized version of the settlers' new lives. In reality, they faced endless hardships—from harsh winters to crop failures to illnesses and death—as they worked to tame a wild land.

Great Britain had peacefully shared Oregon Country since the treaty of 1818, but that peace was now threatened by the growing multitude of Americans who, in the name of Manifest Destiny, were pouring into the Northwest. Their aim was to outnumber the several hundred British settlers there and to overpower them if need be. In 1848, however, the lines of battle dispersed when the two nations signed a pact dividing the area between them. Britain held lands north of the present-day Canadian border, while America claimed those to the south.

Oregon Fever burned through 1846 (1,200 emigrants), 1847 (4,000), and 1848 (1,300). Then, in 1849, the tide ebbed to a trickle of just 450 people. Yet some parts of the trail were busier than ever that year, with close to 26,000 people rising to its challenge. Most of the travelers— an astonishing 25,500—took their wagons only as far as Fort Hall, where they swung southwest along the California Trail. They were infected by a malady even greater than Oregon Fever. Gold had been discovered in California, and they were consumed by the promise of sudden wealth.

In its final miles, the California Trail curled up through the towering Sierra Nevada Mountains.

Five

Tragedy in the Sierras

THE CALIFORNIA TRAIL TOOK SHAPE IN THE 1830s AND EARLY 1840s. IT was forged by a few hunters, adventurers, and pioneers drawn to the vast Mexican province by tales of its rich soil and mild climate. Fine living might be had for anyone daring enough to make the trip.

After dropping southwest into Utah, the California Trail crossed the vast Great Basin Desert to the Humboldt River. It then followed the river until it ran into the rocky face of the Sierra Nevada Mountains. It snaked up through the Sierras' towering heights, and curled down their western slopes to the Sacramento Valley. From there, it moved on to San Francisco.

The 1849 news that gold had been found in the western foothills of the Sierras triggered a wild stampede that sent thousands of people surging along the California Trail. Though the crowds were at their greatest during that rush, the trail had already been used during the decade by

At times in the Sierras, the emigrants had to pull their wagons by hand up steep slopes and over gigantic rock formations.

some seven hundred Americans eager for a new life on the West Coast. The trip was filled with hazards: the Great Basin Desert had to be crossed in the searing heat of summer if the travelers were to scale the Sierras before winter closed in and coated the slopes with snow.

In 1846, word spread of the fate that awaited anyone who became trapped in those heights for the winter: death from starvation and the brutal cold. That was the year that gave the West one of its most tragic incidents—the fate of the Donner Party.

In April 1846, the Donner brothers George and Jacob led a small wagon train out of Illinois along the Oregon Trail. With them were George's wife, his five youngest children, and forty-six-year-old James Reed. With Reed were his wife, their four children, and his wife's mother.

The Donners were prosperous, middle-aged farmers who were well supplied for their journey. They brought saddle horses, cows, beef cattle, and extra oxen for their wagon teams. George and Jacob shared several wagons, and Reed had three, fully stocked with food, clothing, and housewares.

The party reached Fort Bridger in July. There, they made a decision that was to prove fatal. They elected not to travel on to Fort Hall and the junction with the California Trail. Instead, they would now leave the Oregon Trail and head southwest to the Great Salt Lake and then westward to the Humboldt River, and only then connect with the California Trail. It was a shortcut that would lop some four hundred miles off their trek. They had learned of it a year earlier, in a book written by a mountain man named Lansford Hastings.

The Donners and the Reeds left Bridger on July 31. As it turned out, they were not to take the shortcut alone. Other families had entered the fort during their stay. Friendships had been forged and, as a result, several dozen pioneers departed with them.

There was trouble for the expanded party all along the way. First they lost precious time looking for a way around a narrow mountain gorge that blocked their way. Next they had to press through the Great Basin in the terrible heat of summer. They watched it kill more than one hundred of their cattle, saw many of their oxen drop in their tracks, and nervously noted how their food and water were running low.

Years later, one of Reed's children, Virginia, twelve years old at the time of the crossing, wrote a book called *Across the Plains with the Donner Party*. In it, she described the desert:

A dreary, desolate, alkali waste; not a living thing could be seen; it seemed as though the hand of death had been laid upon the land.

She then wrote of a four-day period in which the pioneers, with their own supply almost gone, searched desperately for water:

We started in the evening, traveled all that night and the following day and night—two nights and one day of suffering from thirst and heat by day and piercing cold by night. When the third night fell and we saw the barren waste stretching away apparently as boundless as when we started, my father determined to go ahead in search of water.

He soon returned with word that water was to be found ten miles ahead. That night, with their supply down to just a few drops, the pioneers set out on the ten-mile walk:

Can I ever forget that night in the desert, when we walked mile after mile in the darkness, every step seeming to be the very last we could take! Suddenly all fatigue was banished by fear; through the night came the rushing sound of one of the young steers crazed by thirst and apparently bent upon our destruction. My father, holding his youngest child in his arms and keeping all of us close behind him, drew his pistol, but finally the maddened beast turned and dashed off into the darkness.

The luck of the Reeds seemed to change at that moment, and their long ordeal in the desert soon ended. The emigrants finally reached the Humboldt River and the California Trail in September. The shortcut had saved them no time. It had weakened them and had decimated their livestock, reducing their food supply. Now they stared ahead to the Sierras. They were exhausted, but there was no time for rest. Winter was coming on fast. They had to get over those peaks before the first heavy snows fell.

It was in these tense moments that a new misfortune struck. James Reed and a man named John Snyder, their tempers frayed from exhaustion, got into an argument that ended in Snyder's death when Reed drove a knife into his chest.

Threatened with revenge by Snyder's friends, Reed decided to leave the wagon train. He said a quick goodbye to his family, promised to see them again soon, and rode away with a companion. The two made their way over the Sierras and arrived at Sutter's Fort in late October. Reed began organizing a party to take food back to the people surely trapped in the mountains.

Meanwhile, the Donner wagons were stretched across a meadow-land high in the Sierras, with the first of their number approaching a body of water called Truckee Lake (today Donner Lake). Looming beyond its waters were the rugged slopes that rose to Truckee Pass (Donner Pass), the avenue to the western side of the mountains and the descent to warmth. There was already snow on the slopes, but the pioneers were hopeful that they could get through the pass before more snow blocked their way for the winter.

Three families reached the lake on October 31. They camped overnight and started the climb to Truckee Pass early on November 1.

Long before reaching their goal, they were struggling through snowdrifts five feet deep. The battle was too much for the tired and hungry climbers. They reeled back to the lake.

A storm moved in that night and pelted them with a rain that lasted for hours. On November 3, several more wagons approached through the downpour. The newcomers, with James Reed's family among them, brought the total number of people at the lakeside to sixty. Still far to the rear were the last wagons in the train.

On November 4, under a sky dark with the threat of snow, the lakeside group and their wagons made a new effort to reach Truckee Pass. Virginia Reed recalled the climb years later:

When . . . the wagons could not be dragged through the snow, their goods and provisions were packed on oxen and another start was made, men and women walking in the snow up to their waists, carrying their children in their arms.

One member of the group, Charles Stanton, hiked ahead to the summit. He returned and

Reported that we could get across if we kept right on, but that it would be impossible if snow fell. He was in favor of a forced march until the other side of the summit should be reached, but some of our party were so tired and exhausted with the day's labor that they declared they could not take another step . . . so . . . we camped within three miles of the summit.

That night came the dreaded snow. Around the campfires under the trees great feathery flakes came whirling down. The air was so full of them that one could see objects only a few feet away. . . . We children slept soundly on our cold bed of snow with a soft white mantle falling over us so thickly that every few moments my

After failing to climb through Truckee Pass, one group in the Donner Party returned to Truckee Lake and quickly put up cabins and makeshift shelters for the coming winter.

mother would have to shake the shawl—our only covering—to keep us from being buried alive.

The emigrants, knowing that they were trapped for the winter, returned to Truckee Lake. As shelter for the coming weeks, they built a lean-to and two small cabins. They roofed the cabins over with animal hides.

At this time, stalled by the storm that was lashing the lake, the last wagons in the train were five miles away, at a spot called Alder Creek Valley. There were twenty-one people with the wagons, among them the families of George and Jacob Donner. Like the lakeside party, they built shelters for the winter, quickly nailing up two lean-tos, two cabins, and a tipi.

Imprisoned in the Sierras were eighty-one people—forty adults and forty-one children. They were destined to spend four frozen months in the mountains. In that time, starvation replaced the biting hunger that had been dogging them for weeks. Virginia Reed recalled:

> We now had nothing to eat but raw hides and they were on the roof of the cabin to keep out the snow; when prepared for cooking and boiled, they were simply a pot of glue. . . . Mrs. Breen (a neighbor) prolonged my life by slipping me little bits of meat now and then when she discovered I could not eat the hide.

Virginia also recalled that the storms

> Would often last for ten days at a time, and we would have to cut chips from the logs . . . which formed our cabins, in order to start a fire. We could scarcely walk . . . the men hardly had strength to procure wood. . . . Poor little children were crying with hunger . . . mothers were crying because they had so little to give their children.

Though starving, the lakeside people made several vain attempts to get through Truckee Pass. On December 16, a last try was made. Called the Forlorn Hope Party, ten men, five women, and two boys set out on snowshoes to reach the Sacramento Valley and return with help. With each hiker carrying a blanket and six strips of dried meat, the party managed to struggle through the pass, only to be blinded by a series of blizzards as they staggered down the western slopes. It was during these

The men, women, and boys of the Forlorn Hope Party struggle through the snow in their heroic attempt to reach the Sacramento Valley and summon help for their loved ones trapped high in the mountains.

storms that the story of the Donner Party changed from a tragic story to an ugly one. It became a story of people so desperate with hunger that they turned to a savage practice to survive.

On Christmas Eve, snowshoers William Graves and a friend died of starvation. In his last moments, Graves begged his companions to save themselves by eating his body. It was a plea that they could not bring themselves to obey—at least, not just yet.

Another death struck the party on Christmas Day. Throughout that night, the survivors stared at the body of Patrick Dolan and tried not to think of what must be done to keep from dying. By the next day, they could no longer stand their hunger. Refusing to look at each other, they cut strips of flesh from Dolan's body and roasted them.

The marchers struggled on during the final days of December and the first days of the new year, with death claiming two more victims. Their bodies were cut into strips and eaten.

At last, on January 17, hiker William Eddy staggered into a small settlement at the edge of the Sacramento Valley. He was little more than a skeleton, his face gray, his clothes filthy, his boots gone and his exposed feet frozen and covered with blood. He told the people at the settlement that his companions had given up some miles back and had settled themselves in the snow to await death.

Immediately, a rescue party hurried into the mountains, reaching the remnants of the snowshoe party by following the bloody footprints that Eddy had left in the snow. Brought down to safety were the party's five women and a man. Only seven of the seventeen snowshoers who had started from Truckee Lake had survived.

Four rescue efforts were soon launched from the valley. The first left on February 4 and reached the two Sierra camps at midmonth. The conditions found there sickened the rescuers. Thirteen people were dead, among them Jacob Donner and Eddy's wife and daughter. George Donner lay dying; after cutting his hand while repairing a wagon at Alder Creek

Valley, he had ignored the wound, only to have it become infected; now it was rotting with deadly gangrene. The people who were still alive were skeletons and seemed to be going insane. There was grisly evidence that, like the Forlorn Hope Party, they had survived by eating the dead.

The rescuers could safely take away twenty-one survivors. As they made their way down to the Sacramento Valley, they met a second group of rescuers, with James Reed at its head. After weeks spent organizing a rescue team, he was at last coming for his family. He caught sight of his wife and two of their children. After a brief but poignant reunion, he hurried on, arriving at the two camps in late March.

Reed and his team gathered seventeen people strong enough to make the hike to safety. They successfully put Truckee Pass behind them, but were then pinned down for three days by a snowstorm of hurricane force. George Donner's five-year-old son died soon after they ran out of food.

The third rescue team reached the Sierra camps at the end of March. The rescuers found that William Eddy's son had died and been eaten. They took the three sons of George Donner away. Donner, attended by his wife, was too sick to move and stayed behind to die. Only one person remained alive—a man named Lewis Keseberg—when the fourth and final team reached Truckee Lake in April.

It was then that a final death count could be made. Of the seventy-nine Donner Party pioneers who had been trapped that terrible winter, thirty-seven men, women, and children had lost their lives. Their fate would now serve as a dark warning of the dangers that lay in wait for those who ventured into the mountains of the Far West at the wrong time of year.

Newspaper reports of the discovery of gold in California were avidly read by people throughout the world and triggered a massive rush westward in early 1849.

Six

Sailing for the Gold

THE RUMORS AND REPORTS WERE FANTASTIC. THEY HAD BEEN SPREADING across the country all of 1848 and seemed beyond belief. They held that gold had been discovered in January at a sawmill owned by John Sutter in California's Sierra foothills and that it was to be found everywhere— on the ground, among the rocks, and in streambeds, where you scooped it up in metal pans. All you had to do to get rich was to go out there and start looking.

People everywhere, not only in the United States but also in Europe and China, gazed hungrily at California. They would drop everything in a minute and race there if only those rumors and reports were true. But were they? They were so fantastic.

There was an October 1848 letter that was printed in two newspapers, the Missouri *Statesman* and the Independence *Expositor*. It was written by M. T. McClellan, who had brought his family west earlier that year:

My little girls can make from 5 to 25 dollars per day washing gold in pans. . . . My average income this winter will be about $150 a day, and if I should strike a good lead it will be a great deal more.

These were stunning sums for workers in the mid-1800s. Far more stunning was the figure given in a letter to another Missouri newspaper, the *Republican*. It was written by Peter H. Burnett:

The gold is positively inexhaustible. One hundred millions will be taken out annually in the course of two years . . .

Two news reports turned the rumors into fact at year's end. First, on December 5, President James K. Polk announced that they could be believed. U.S. government officers in the West had seen the gold for themselves.

Then, two days later, the newspapers reported that a leather pouch had arrived at the nation's capital from California. It contained 280 ounces of high quality gold.

That was enough for the gold-hungry everywhere. Loosed in early 1849 was a stampede west. In the vanguard were hundreds of ships of all types—from whalers and merchantmen to fishing boats and coastal steamers. They were all put to work reaping the fortune in fares paid by the eager gold seekers. They were to carry some 100,000 passengers to California in the next few years.

As was true of the westward-bound wagon trains, both men and women traveled to California by sea. Some of the women were married to ships' officers. Others traveled with their husbands—and perhaps children—and some went alone in search of a new life for themselves.

This Currier and Ives lithograph The Way to California *depicts the various transports—from the practical to the fantastic—that would take a gold seeker to the riches of the Sierras. A large ship sails off, leaving desperate would-be passengers on the dock.*

The idea of sailing to California was especially popular among the gold seekers coming from the East Coast of the United States or western Europe. There was no need for them to struggle across the continent in a covered wagon. They could book passage west at any seaport between Maine in the north and the city of New Orleans in the south.

Further, ships offered a great advantage over the covered wagons. They could set sail in the winter months. Wagon trains could not push off until the spring thaw melted the mountain snows in their path. Then

John A. Sutter

Born in Germany in 1803, John Augustus Sutter was an ambitious merchant who came looking for wealth in America in 1834. After working for five years in New Mexico, Oregon, and Hawaii, he arrived in California.

The rotund adventurer quickly saw how he could make a fortune in this wide-open land. He could become rich by farming and ranching—and richer still by building a trading post to serve the Americans who were beginning to arrive from the East.

Turning these ideas into a reality, he took out Mexican citizenship, a step that enabled him to secure a land grant of 49,000 acres in the Sacramento Valley. Here, he fashioned an empire for himself, planting his crops, grazing his cattle, and building his trading post, which he called New Helvetia (New Switzerland) for his parents' birthplace.

The trading post was soon serving as a center for the early settlers, traders, and trappers who had made their way to California. It then became famous the world over as Sutter's Fort, when gold was discovered on a section of his property on January 24, 1848.

At first, Sutter was dizzy with the thought that the gold would make him one of the world's richest men in the world. The precious metal was his, and his alone, because it had been found on his land. But he was overwhelmed by hordes of fortune hunters swarming over his land. They simply ignored his claim to the riches. Then, when many of their number failed to strike it rich, they settled on the land and started farms, depriving him of prime acreage. Making matters worse, most of his workers abandoned his trading post and fields and went looking for gold, leaving his crops to wither and die. His trading post lost more and more business as the city of Sacramento took shape around it, crowded with stores that offered wares that he alone had once sold. In just two years, he was a ruined, poverty-stricken man.

After California became a state in 1850, Sutter tried to regain some of his wealth. He asked Congress to pay him for his lost land and for the help his fort had given to so many settlers. Congress turned him down on the grounds that his acreage had been obtained from a foreign nation and that, as a consequence, he had no claim against the United States government.

Sutter stubbornly continued to seek repayment for the rest of his life, but in vain. He died in poverty in 1880 at the age of seventy-seven.

Charles Nahl painted the sawmill where John Marshall, one of John Sutter's employees, discovered gold in 1848.

they needed at least five months to reach their destination. The sea travelers felt sure they would be rolling in riches while the wagons were still on the road.

Let's imagine that you're a forty-niner—as the people in the rush were nicknamed—who has decided to travel by ship. The idea of sailing to California holds no fear for you. You are not venturing into an unknown sea. American ships, along with British vessels, have been entering the Pacific and landing in Oregon to take on cargoes of furs since the late 1700s. California's coast is also no secret, even though Americans were not allowed to trade there when the Spanish held the region. But then, as happened in New Mexico, outsiders were welcomed when the Mexicans ousted the Spaniards in 1820. U.S. ships are now a familiar sight at landings all along the coast.

Further, this is 1849. Just as you're not plunging into an uncharted sea so are you not sailing to some strange, foreign destination. California is now an American territory, having been won along with New Mexico in the Mexican War of 1846–1848. In fact, the Treaty of Guadalupe Hidalgo, which formally ended the war and turned California into a territory, was signed just nine days after gold was discovered at Sutter's sawmill. Next year—on September 9, 1850—California will become the nation's thirty-first state.

Having decided to sail to the gold fields, you choose one of the two sea routes west. The first will carry you far down the Atlantic, then west past the foot of South America, and north to California for a landing at San Francisco. The voyage will last about six months, cover some 13,000 miles, and cost you between three hundred and five hundred dollars.

The second route, which is in the same price range, takes you to the east coast of the Isthmus of Panama for a forty-one-mile hike across to Panama City on the Pacific, there to be picked up by another ship for the final run to San Francisco. The trip will save you three months of travel time, but will take you through a jungle ripe with the threat of yellow fever.

Clipper ships were among the hundreds of vessels that made the rapid sea runs to California.

Because of the number of forty-niners at sea, you travel in crowded conditions, no matter your route. They will prove especially uncomfortable on the long South American run. Not lucky enough to book one of the few staterooms with berths for two to four passengers, you find yourself in a small cabin nailed together on deck for the voyage.

Pioneer Edwin Ayers was assigned such a cabin in 1849 and wrote that it measured just "14 by 20 feet, with 18 double bunks for thirty-six

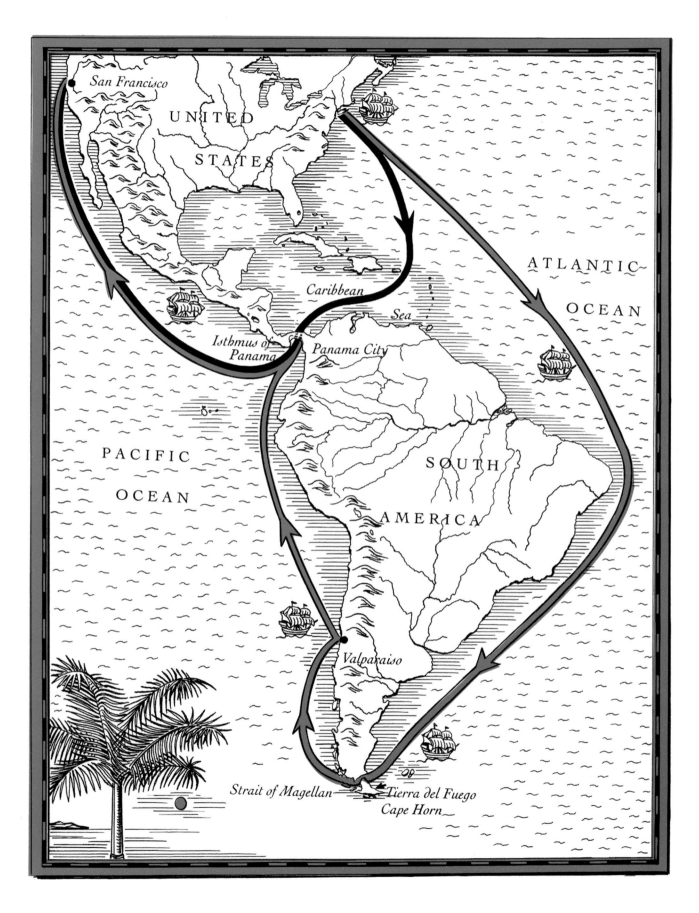

San Francisco

UNITED

STATES

Caribbean

Sea

ATLANTIC

OCEAN

Isthmus of
Panama

Panama City

PACIFIC

OCEAN

SOUTH

AMERICA

Valparaiso

Strait of Magellan

Tierra del Fuego

Cape Horn

men to sleep and live in." But Ayers was luckier than those who traveled by steerage and were packed into the open spaces between decks, which one passenger described as "damp and dirty" and where "the 'oniony' smell . . . is enough to vomit a horse."

Along with the crowded conditions, you find shipboard food hard to take. It is a constant source of complaint, as can be seen in passenger Richard Hale's 1849 description:

> The usual fare is hard baked biscuit, called by the sailors 'hard-tack,' baked very hard to prevent moulding, and beef as salty as salt itself, named in sea language 'salt junk' and 'salt-horse,' with 'duff' or boiled pudding, served once a week, and a hash when they are fortunate enough to have potatoes.

You live through a wide range of experiences during the long weeks at sea. First, there is the seasickness that makes life miserable until you grow accustomed to the roll of the ship. Then there is the fun of getting acquainted with your fellow passengers and finding that they come from all walks of life. You learn to pass the time in various ways: you write letters home for later mailing; you play checkers and various card games; you attend the evening sing-alongs and banjo and fiddle concerts out on deck.

All these activities finally fall prey to one problem—the boredom that comes from all those weeks at sea. You now do anything you can think of to pass the time. For example, one traveler wrote that he went into his cabin one day and "opened my box and spread all its contents out on my bunk, examining each article carefully and then stowing it away again."

A friend, on happening by, decided to open his own trunk, remove its contents, and then replace them in the same order as before. Both agreed that it was a pleasant way to waste an afternoon.

Boredom disappears when the Atlantic's storms first hit you. They

These passengers aboard a steamer bound for California via the Isthmus of Panama were among the luckier travelers. They had staterooms that accommodated from two to four people. Most passengers were jammed into small cabins (with as many as thirty-six travelers to a cabin) or given bunks in open, foul-smelling spaces between decks.

are vicious and have the power to splinter a ship. According to a passenger, one storm in 1850 was frightening in the day but terrifying at night:

Impenetrable darkness surrounded us, relieved only by sheets of white foam dashing over the bows, as the doomed ship madly plunged into the angry waters. When one sea more powerful than another would strike her, causing her to tremble in every timber, I would grasp my chair, shut my eyes, and think that we were fast being engulfed in the sea. . . . Never, through all the vicissitudes of after life, will one thought, one feeling, then endured, fade from the volume of memory.

The writer was Mrs. D. B. Bates, the wife of the captain of the beleaguered ship. The storm lasted for a week.

Boredom also vanishes when you swing west for the struggle into the Pacific. And a struggle it always is—a battle that is staged on either of two fronts. First, your captain may sail well south of the South American mainland, move past the giant island of Tierra del Fuego, and then turn west to travel past Cape Horn into the Pacific. Or he may press west through the Strait of Magellan, which runs between the South American coast and Tierra del Fuego.

Suppose he chooses to fight his way past Cape Horn. Vicious winds constantly whip the sea into giant waves that, on breaking, plummet down on the ship and send tons of water crashing through cabins and holds. Freezing water coats the decks, sails, and rigging with ice. The ship loses headway, turns away in defeat, and limps back into the Atlantic. Then it stubbornly swings about for another try. One vessel took five weeks in 1849 to make its way past the cape.

If the captain fears that the cape will be too much for his ship, he turns into the Strait of Magellan. This is a somewhat safer route to the Pacific because the winds here are not so vicious. But there is still a great

An artist's rendition of five steamers that were lost during a sixty-day period in 1853 while trying to sail from the Atlantic to the Pacific. Two were destroyed by internal explosions.

danger: violent storms can hit you without warning and rip away your sails and spars. Or the thick fogs that routinely blanket the area can blind you. Either hazard can send you crashing into the rocky shores that line the waterway. All too easily, you can suffer the fate that befell a schooner in late 1849. After blundering ashore in a fog, she was described by traveler Benjamin Bourne from the deck of a passing ship:

We noticed the wreck of a new vessel, lying well up on the shore, her bottom badly shattered by the rocks on which she had been driven, and both masts gone. . . . On the opposite shore were parts of iron-mills, and other machinery, probably designed for use in California. The shore was strewed with trunks and chests from the wreck; she had been stripped of everything valuable.

Once you reach the Pacific, you slowly beat your way north, stopping to take on supplies at Valparaiso, Chile, and the Isthmus of Panama. At Panama City, you see throngs of people on its beaches. They have just trudged across the isthmus and are waiting to catch the ship that will take them to San Francisco.

Now let's suppose that you're destined to be one of those people on the beach. You decide to travel via the isthmus. After crossing the Caribbean Sea, you make port at the village of Colon on Panama's east coast.

You go ashore near the Chagres River and are greeted with the ramshackle spectacle of Colon's several dozen bamboo huts and two rickety hotels. While staying there, you can either camp on the beach or crowd into a room with other travelers at one of the hotels. And you can either cook your own meals or buy dinners of iguana or monkey at the hotels.

The first leg of the isthmus crossing takes you along the Chagres River to the villages of Cruces and Gorgona in the low mountains that run down the spine of Panama. The villages lie just twenty-one miles away, but a trip of two to three days is needed to reach them. You travel in either a canoe or a *bungo*, a hollowed-out mahogany log that measures between fifteen and twenty-five feet. Both are paddled by Panamanians.

You pass along waters alive with alligators and through a jungle throbbing with screeching birds, monkeys, snakes, and countless insects. The air is humid and the daytime temperatures soar above a sweltering 100 degrees Fahrenheit. Despite these problems, most of your companions

San Francisco grew from a tiny village to a bustling city in a matter of months. This photograph called "Forest of Masts Panorama" shows the city in 1851. Ships that had

do not complain. They insist that they are having a great adventure.

When the river voyage ends, you rent a mule for the ride down the Pacific side of the isthmus to Panama City. At first, the ride terrifies you. The trail is so narrow that there is barely enough room for the animal to move. A single misstep will surely pitch the two of you off the trail and send you tumbling down a steep slope and into the tangled jungle. But the animal steps confidently from rock to rock and past one hole after another. He is the most sure-footed beast you've ever seen. You come to trust him and begin to relax and enjoy the wild scenery on all sides.

The crossing ends on the beach at Panama City. The sands are

carried gold seekers to California were abandoned in the harbor when their crews hurried off to the Sierras in quest of quick riches.

thronged with men, women, and children, all waiting for sea passage to San Francisco. The passage is to be provided by a newly formed company. It operates several coastal steamers that shuttle back and forth between the isthmus and San Francisco. If all goes well, you'll be on your way in about two weeks. From San Francisco, you'll head up the Sacramento River to Sutter's Fort and the gold fields.

While you have been challenging the sea, covered wagons have been moving west out of Missouri. We join them now on that most traveled pathway of all—the overland route.

St. Joseph, Missouri, a chief starting point for the wagons heading beyond the frontier.

Seven

By Wagon Train to California

IT'S THE SPRING OF 1850. YOU ARE JOINING THE GREAT MIGRATION WEST. You may be racing to California with dreams of striking it rich in a Sierra mining camp. Or seeking some land to farm. Or hoping to start a business of your own.

Whatever the reason for your decision, you no longer need to start from Independence, Missouri, unless you wish to do so. Several other towns have joined it as gateways to the Far West. Strung along the Missouri River are Council Bluffs, Iowa; Fort Leavenworth, Kansas; Omaha, Nebraska; and the most used of all, St. Joseph, Missouri.

The streets are jammed with emigrants when you arrive in St. Joe, as everyone calls it. Your reaction to the town is likely the same as that of twelve-year-old Sallie Hester, when she and her parents came here last year:

As far as the eye can reach, so great is the emigration, you see nothing but wagons. This town presents a striking appearance—a vast army on wheels—crowds of men, women, and lots of children and last but not least the cattle and horses on which our lives depend.

Your wagon, like most others, is a small rectangular wooden box about four feet wide and between ten and twelve feet long. An arched white cover of canvas is stretched across strips of hickory wood. The box is mounted on spoked wheels with iron tires. Attached to its front is a "jockey box" loaded with hand tools. Hanging from the rear is a "grease bucket" filled with a mixture of tar and tallow to lubricate the wheels.

Your wagon must be both durable and lightweight, strong enough to handle the rough trail ahead while carrying more than a ton of supplies, but light enough not to exhaust the animals that must pull it day after day.

Most of your fellow pioneers have teams of four or more oxen and several mules. The oxen are used because they can survive by foraging grass along the trail. The mules require that sacks of feed be carried for them, but they will more than earn their keep when they make their sure-footed way across the Rockies and the Sierras. In addition to the teams, you have brought along cattle for food and milk.

Most wagons not only look alike, they are packed alike, too. This is because everyone has invested in the same guidebooks for the journey. The books have been written by men who have either scouted the route themselves or talked with those who have. Most advise that you carry at least 150 pounds of flour, twenty-five pounds each of sugar, salt, and bacon, and fifteen pounds of coffee. In addition, you should bring along tea, cornmeal, dried beans, an oven, a butter churn, pots, dishes, firearms, and ammunition—in all, supplies enough to survive the months of travel as well as the time you'll need to find a spot for farming or digging for gold.

The wagon boxes, often just four feet wide and from ten to twelve feet long, were packed so full with precious family possessions that little room was left for the pioneers themselves.

Suppose that you're not out just to grab some gold and dash home but are planning to settle in the West. You're sure to have household treasures crammed into your wagon—the family Bible, portraits of loved ones, a few pieces of furniture. All is tightly packed, leaving scant room for you and your family.

At last, it's early May and you can make a start. The snow has melted. Now is your best chance of getting over the Sierras before next winter's snows begin to fall. Your train crosses the Missouri River and advances at about twenty miles a day through the rolling lands of Kansas and then Nebraska.

Each day's journey is made in two short trips. The first begins at dawn and continues through the morning until a stop is made for "nooning"—a two-hour period in which the livestock graze and the pioneers have a midday meal and a rest. The train then moves on until a final stop at sunset.

The evening is first spent cooking and, if necessary, doing such chores as wagon repairs. Then it's time to relax in any number of ways. There are quiet conversations about home and the future. There are sewing bees for the women, card games for the men, hide-and-seek for the children, and shy flirtations and quiet walks together for the young people who have met each other during the weeks since St. Joe. There are often sing-alongs to the accompaniment of banjos and fiddles. And dances for those with the energy after a day on the trail.

These first weeks in Kansas and Nebraska are a pleasure. There is fine grass for the animals, ample water, and plenty of wood for the cook fires. Best of all, there are fascinating sights at every step. In Kansas, you glimpse your first buffalo, peaceful giants that weigh a ton or more. When they run in vast herds across the distant horizon, the sound of their hooves rolls over you like thunder and vibrates the ground underfoot.

Then there is the day when a band of mounted Indians blocks the trail and, with great dignity, demands that you pay a toll—perhaps food

An armed chief has brought a wagon train to a halt. He will most likely let it pass when the wagon master offers to pay him a toll—usually food or animals—for the right to cross tribal land.

Sweet Betsy from Pike

John A. Stone was a colorful character who went to California in search of gold in 1850. Empty-handed after three years of fruitless digging, he turned to composing and singing. Under the name Old Put, he became the singing voice of the gold rush. In 1858 he published a collection of some of his best-known songs in a volume entitled *Put's Golden Songster*, which included the adventures of "Sweet Betsy from Pike." By setting Betsy's exploits to a tune that everyone already knew—the British music hall favorite "Villikins and His Dinah"—Stone ensured that his listeners would be humming his song after a first hearing. And people have been humming, and singing, it ever since.

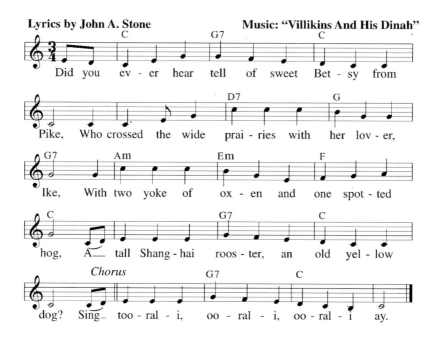

Lyrics by John A. Stone　　　　**Music: "Villikins And His Dinah"**

Did you ev-er hear tell of sweet Bet-sy from Pike, Who crossed the wide prai-ries with her lov-er, Ike, With two yoke of ox-en and one spot-ted hog, A— tall Shang-hai roos-ter, an old yel-low dog?

Chorus

Sing— too-ral-i, oo-ral-i, oo-ral-i ay.

The shanghai ran off and their cattle all died,
That morning the last piece of bacon was fried;
Poor Ike was discouraged and Betsy got mad,
The dog drooped his tail and looked wondrously sad. Chorus

They stopped at Salt Lake to inquire the way
When Brigham declared that sweet Betsy should stay;
But Betsy got frightened and ran like a deer,
While Brigham stood pawing the ground like a steer. Chorus

They soon reached the desert, where Betsy gave out,
And down in the sand she lay rolling about;
While Ike, half distracted, looked on with surprise,
Saying, "Betsy, get up, you'll get sand in your eyes." Chorus

Sweet Betsy got up in a great deal of pain,
Declared she'd go back to Pike County again;
But Ike gave a sign, and they fondly embraced,
And they traveled along with his arm 'round her waist. Chorus

One evening quite early they camped on the Platte,
'Twas near by the road on a green shady flat,
Where Betsy, sore-footed, lay down to repose,
With wonder Ike gazed on that Pike County rose. Chorus

Their wagons broke down with a terrible crash,
And out on the prairie rolled all kinds of trash;
A few little baby clothes done up with care,
'Twas rather suspicious, though all on the square. Chorus

They suddenly stopped on a very high hill,
With wonder looked down upon old Placerville;
Ike sighed when he said, and he cast his eyes down,
"Sweet Betsy, my darling, we've got to Hangtown." Chorus

or animals—for the right to graze their land and drink their water. Others approach you during stops, some to shake your hand out of curiosity and some to trade buffalo robes for household wares. Or you may be joined for a time by a troup of braves, as was the emigrant who signed his writings with the initials M.M.G.:

Yesterday we fell in with a party of eighteen Sioux and Cheyenne warriors . . . armed with guns, bows, shields, and spears. Their appearance, no doubt, made many a "Green 'un" tremble with fear. They were on the warpath for the Pawnees, the scalps of two of whom they had dangling at their saddle bows.

You are lucky that the gold rush is still new. The Native Americans pretty much leave you alone, though you are always in danger of having your livestock stolen. In general, they see you as visitors who are simply passing through their lands and are content to let you go on your way. Only later will they realize that the white newcomers are swallowing their lands. Then there will be bloodshed.

Indians are not the only fascinating people along the trail. Now and again, a strange gold seeker startles everyone, as did the traveler who was sighted one day this year at Fort Laramie, Wyoming. A writer at the fort described him as

The "wheel barrow man" who dropped upon us yesterday. He left St. Joseph about twenty-five days ago carrying his all in a light wheel barrow, and has out-stripped almost everything on the road. He appeared in high spirits and felt confident that he would be the first man in the "diggings" by this route . . . and then pushed on to the tune of Yankee Doodle towards the setting sun.

All this is not to say that the journey goes smoothly every step of the way. Each day brings some sort of trouble. A horse stumbles into a patch of quicksand while fording Nebraska's North Platte River. The rider is thrown into the water and almost drowns before his friends can drag him ashore. Wagon breakdowns, mostly broken wheels and axles, cause hours of delay while repairs are made.

And almost daily, there are accidents. A man breaks his arm while replacing a broken wheel. The driver loses control of a wagon as it is going downhill; his wife is killed when she is thrown clear. Many of the accidents involve children, such as the one recorded by ten-year-old Mary Ackley:

My two brothers were playing in the wagon on the bed, the curtains [the sides of the wagon's canvas cover] were rolled up and the wheels went down in a rut which jarred the wagon, throwing brother John out. A hind wheel ran over him, breaking one of his legs.

(Brother John was seven years old. Mary added that he "was confined to the wagon for the rest of the long journey.")

Worst of all, the cholera that has long gripped the East and the Midwest is stalking the train, terrorizing everyone with its ability to kill in a matter of hours. It is a common occurrence for a man, woman, or child to awaken in fine health in the morning, fall ill by midday, and lie dead by sunset. Daily, the train stops and the people gather together in silence while graves are dug and funeral services held. They will continue to do so until the cholera burns itself out up ahead in Wyoming.

In Nebraska, you stop for several days at Fort Kearny, named for General Stephen Kearny, a hero of the Mexican War. Then, as you approach the future state's western frontier, you are struck with the splendor of two natural formations: first, awesome Chimney Rock, a granite spire that rises more than five hundred feet above the trail, and then even

Artist William Henry Jackson sketched this wagon train struggling through a violent thunderstorm on the Nebraska prairie.

more awesome Scotts Bluff with its spectacular rocky tiers. It has the look of a mighty city looming high above your head.

On leaving Scotts Bluff, you enter Wyoming. For days now, the grassy plains and wooded areas of the Midwest have been gradually disappearing, making way for a high, scrub-covered desert. You are faced with a new problem. There is no longer ample wood for your cook fires. Your cooking must now be done with a disgusting fuel—the droppings left by the buffalo herds known as "buffalo chips." They are easy to find and give off a fine heat, but everyone hates them, so much that someone has written this sarcastic song:

It's fun to cook with buffalo chips,
Take one that's newly born.
If I knew once what I know now,
I'd have gone around the Horn.

Once inside Wyoming, you stop briefly at Fort Laramie. From there, you move on to central Wyoming for yet another breathtaking landmark, one that lies like a giant loaf of bread on a treeless plain and measures about a mile around its base. This is Independence Rock, so named because explorer-trapper William Sublette came upon it on July 4 back in 1830 and celebrated that year's Independence Day in its shadow. Like the travelers who have already been here, you climb the rock and leave your name carved in granite for all future passersby to see.

In Wyoming, you are on ground that is rising into the Rocky Mountains. The air thins and the nights turn frigid as you climb higher and higher. Finally, you're at 7,500 feet and moving along a gently rising avenue of wild grass. Your wagon is rumbling and creaking up South Pass, the famous roadway through the Rockies. From here, you will move on to Fort Bridger and then to Fort Hall, just across the border into Idaho.

During the miles to the fort you will suffer increasingly from a problem that has been irritating you for days—the mosquito. The buzzing insect was mentioned twice in the journal that two friends, Vincent Geiger and Wakeman Bryarly, kept of their journey west:

The musquitoes [sic] were larger & more numerous here than any place we have yet passed. . . . They were so thick you could reach out and get your hand-full. We tried to tie up our heads and faces, but they would creep in wherever an opening was left. Our horses & mules were literally covered with them & you could scrape them off by handfulls.

Some miles beyond Fort Hall, you swing onto the California Trail and begin the most dangerous part of your journey.

The California Trail drops southwest through miles of sagebrush and enters Utah. You have reached the Great Basin, some 200,000 square miles of burning sand and clay that stretches over five hundred miles out to the foot of the Sierras in the future state of Nevada.

The hike across the Utah desert is difficult in the broiling heat. The sand becomes so hot that, as happened to Geiger and Bryarly, it burns through the soles of your boots and blisters your feet. But things are even worse when you enter Nevada and come to the Humboldt River. The river is to be a deadly enemy for the 350 miles that you will now follow it toward the Sierras.

Why? Because its waters are heavily laced with alkali. When you cannot keep the livestock from drinking it, they soon collapse and die. You and your fellow pioneers boil the water before daring to touch it. But still you suffer the agonizing cramps and terrible embarrassment of dysentery.

Quite as dangerous as its alkali content is the river's ever more sluggish character as it moves along its course. Each day, it loses more of its greenish color, turning a dirty coffee brown before its murky water forms

In this William Henry Jackson painting, wagon trains approach awe-inspiring Chimney Rock, which rises some five hundred feet above the trail.

a bog—a trap for any thirsty animal that blunders into it. The danger was described by emigrant A. M. Williams in 1851: "We would pass every day from fifty to a hundred horses, mules, and oxen mired in the boggy and spungy bottom of the Humboldt left to struggle for a few days in the mud and then die."

Just as the river is draining away to mud, so are your supplies running low. Each day you eat as little as possible and take just a few sips of boiled water. You plod out into the river to cut reeds and bring them back to feed the livestock. All the while, you move in a daze through the terrible heat.

July turns into August. Daily, the temperatures soar to between 100 and 106 degrees Fahrenheit. The heat exacts a terrible toll on your companions. There are deaths, especially among the very old and very young. One traveler goes insane with the heat and has to be tied down in the bed of his wagon. Another says that he can go no farther; he sits at trailside, ignores all pleas to stand again, and watches the train slowly vanish beyond the heat shimmering up from the dusty earth.

Some families now moan that they made a terrible mistake in coming west. A few, as others have done in the past months, turn back for home. Others say that they have come too far to retreat but wonder if there will ever be an end to their journey other than death.

There will. But first you must conquer the worst stretch of land your trip has to offer. Late in August, the Humboldt finally disappears, its brown waters swallowed up by the earth. The Sierras, with the Truckee River flowing at their base, loom more than forty miles away, just beyond a desert in which not a single drop of water is to be found. To avoid dying of thirst, you must make a nonstop dash to the Truckee. There is no time to rest.

The dash is a horror. You start in the coolness of night, but the sun rises and by midday has begun to fell the oxen and horses with its merciless heat. They must be left behind to die. To help the surviving animals, families empty their wagons. Hurled away, as emigrant Solomon Gorgas wrote of his journey, are "clothing of the best and worst kind . . . quilts, kettles, bake pots, cooking utensils, stoves without number, tents . . . " Wagons left without a team to pull them are simply abandoned.

The castoffs join the litter that preceding trains have left behind. Almost the entire distance to the Truckee is lined with dead animals (creating an almost unbearable stench) and once-dear possessions that are now useless junk. Most heartbreaking of all are your fellow pioneers who die and must be left at trailside, some buried and some not.

But the dash across what everyone now calls the "Forty Mile Desert" finally ends at the Truckee River (or the nearby Carson River for some travelers). You breathe a prayer of thanks. Yes, you are exhausted, hungry, and sick, with most of your life's possessions lying somewhere back in the dust. But life-giving water is once again at hand. Best of all, you are at the foot of the Sierras and it is not yet September. The first snows of winter are yet to come. A backbreaking climb—a final test of your spirit and strength—lies ahead. But, having struggled this far and won, you know that you are certain to survive. The fate that awaited the Donners is not to be yours.

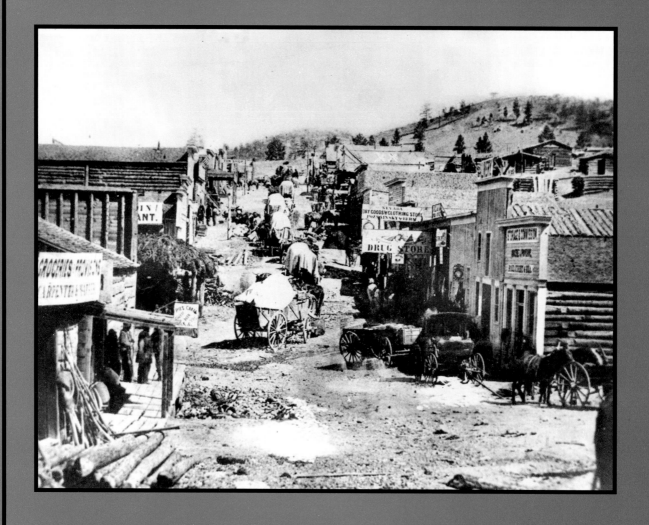

In the wake of the California gold rush, the precious metal was found in other regions and lured new floods of emigrants west. This 1865 photograph captures the main street of Helena, Montana, which sprang up during a major strike. The town became the state's capital in 1875.

Eight

Into the Future

THE CALIFORNIA GOLD RUSH LASTED FROM 1849 TO 1853. IT BEGAN TO fade when the system for collecting the gold underwent a change. At first, a miner could gather dust and nuggets from streams and rivers, where they had been deposited by the erosion of the surrounding earth. But soon these "easy pickins" ran out and far greater riches were found in underground veins. The mining of the veins was a process too costly for the individual miner, who was forced to step aside for wealthy corporations. The wild days of the rush were over.

Even when the stampede lost its impetus, the migration continued. Settlers were lured to the Far West by the opportunities it promised for ranching, farming, and business. In addition, the reports of other ore strikes—silver and gold along Nevada's Comstock Lode and gold in Colorado, Montana, Wyoming, and South Dakota—acted like giant magnets, drawing thousands of adventurers between the 1850s and the late 1870s.

Of the routes west, the overland trail continued to be the busiest of all throughout the 1850s. As mentioned earlier, it is estimated that 350,000 people made their way along the route between 1840 and 1869. Some 238,000 are said to have used the road in the 1850s, with 39,000 heading for Oregon. The California and Utah travelers are lumped together and set at around 198,500.

Though thousands made their way successfully into the Far West, thousands of others lost their lives in the effort. The exact number who perished along the various trails is unknown, but historians believe that the overland route alone took as many as 30,000 lives. Chiefly to blame for the deaths were cholera and illnesses stemming from poor sanitation, rotting food, and bad water; accidents, which were as varied as they were tragic; and the rigors of the journey, which most often claimed the lives of the very young and the very old.

Perhaps the most graphic of all the estimates holds that the deaths along the overland route added up to one grave about every five hundred feet.

What happened to those who successfully reached their destinations? Many were greeted with bitter disappointment. This was especially true of the forty-niners who did not reach the Sierras until late in the gold rush. They found a place whose waterways had been picked clean of dust and nuggets by the first arrivals and whose underground veins were now being mined by companies with costly drilling equipment.

Some of the early arrivals went home with small fortunes, others with empty pockets. Still others, either with or without winnings in the Sierras, stayed on to farm, to find work, or to start businesses of their own. Some made fortunes without slaving in the gold camps. One of their number was a young merchant who decided to manufacture work pants for the miners—Levi Strauss.

Life was tough for the pioneer families who carved farms from the wilds.

Of all the emigrants, the farmers probably had the most difficult lives, even in those regions such as Oregon and California that were said to be especially fertile. Wherever they settled, they faced the job of transforming a wilderness into productive acreage. They felled trees (where there were trees) to make way for their fields. They tilled those fields, planted their crops, and nursed them to fruition, always with the threat that all their work could be ruined by a sudden storm or drought. And they built their own homes—log and clapboard cabins in wooded regions; tar paper shacks, sod houses (made of earthen blocks), and dugouts where wood was scarce or nonexistent.

Though many sod houses were cut into hillsides, here is one that stood by itself in the middle of the Nebraska plains. Note the sod bricks that form the walls and roof. Photograph taken around 1890.

The dugouts were the most primitive form of housing. To build one, a family began by digging into a hillside and removing the earth to form the floor of a room measuring about fourteen feet by fourteen feet. The hillside served as the dugout's back wall while a front wall was erected of sod bricks, with spaces left open for a window and door. The job was finished off with a grass roof. The family then lived with the certainty that the roof would leak with every rain and the fear that an animal—perhaps the family cow—would blunder onto it one day and come crashing down on everyone.

The work of farming was exhausting for all family members—mother, father, children, and grandparents alike. Mary Walker, who settled in Oregon in the late 1830s, described what life must have been like for pioneer women everywhere when she wrote in her diary:

Rose about five. Had breakfast. Got my house work done about nine. Baked six loaves of bread. Made a kettle of Mush and now have a suet pudding and beef boiling. I have managed to put my clothes away and set my house in order.

She then finished the entry with:

Nine o'clock p.m. was delivered of another son.

Mrs. Walker gave birth to eight children while living on the frontier, often without the help of a doctor or midwife.

The migration to the Far West was a triumph for the pioneers and the legions of Americans who believed deeply in the concept of Manifest Destiny. But it was a tragedy for the Native Americans who stood in the path of the thousands who came sweeping into their lands first by covered wagon and later, in the wake of the Civil War, via a growing network of railroads.

At first, the Indians dealt peacefully with the United States government. Treaties were made that set aside great tracts of land—called reservations—for the tribes. But the pacts were soon broken when the lands were needed for settlement and development. The treachery angered the Indians and festered into outright rage as the years passed.

At last, the rage burst into rebellion. In 1862, when federal troops were called away from the Sioux reservation to fight in the Civil War, the tribe went on the warpath, killed dozens of white settlers, and attacked a federal fort in Minnesota. State militia and volunteer troops quickly crushed the uprising. In its wake, thirty-eight of the Sioux braves were hanged, the largest mass execution in U.S. history.

Though crushed, the rebellion ignited uprisings everywhere—by the Cheyenne and Sioux in the Dakotas, the Modoc in California, the Apache in New Mexico and Arizona, the Comanche and Kiowa in Texas, and the Arapaho in Montana and Wyoming. The fighting reached its peak in the mid-1870s when gold was discovered in the Black Hills of South Dakota and thousands of miners came rushing onto lands that were reserved for the Sioux. Furious over the invasion and over the news that crews were about to survey the reservation lands in preparation for building the Northern Pacific Railroad, some three thousand warriors (both Sioux and members of neighboring tribes) gathered at an encampment along Montana's Little Bighorn River. There, led by Chief Sitting Bull and Crazy Horse, they stood ready to fend off the onslaught. It came in June 1876, with the arrival of a large federal force. One cavalry unit of 264 men under Colonel George A. Custer rashly attacked the 3,000-strong encampment on the twenty-fifth of the month. He and his troops were wiped out in less than an hour.

The Sioux did not enjoy their victory for long. Thousands of U.S. troops, all determined to avenge the Custer massacre, came rushing into

An early farm hugs the shore of Puget Sound in Washington. The pioneers of the great western migration claimed the land far beyond what had once been the American frontier. By 1912, the United States stretched west from the Atlantic to the Pacific and south from Canada to Mexico.

the region. Outnumbered and with little food, the Sioux were forced to surrender and return to their reservation.

Even then, the fighting did not end. It continued in various parts of the West, with the Sioux rising again and carrying on as best they could in South Dakota until 1890. In that year, they suffered their final defeat in the massacre at Wounded Knee Creek. By then, further resistance to the white tide was recognized as futile.

Though the great westward migration was at its height in the 1840s and 1850s, it continued to attract streams of settlers throughout the rest of the nineteenth century. Before they were done, those emigrants—from hunters, trappers, and traders to gold seekers, farmers, ranchers, and business people—had reached all the lands west of Missouri and had paved the way for their admission into the Union—Texas, 1845; California, 1850; Oregon, 1859; Kansas, 1861; Nevada, 1864; Nebraska, 1867; Colorado, 1876; Washington, Montana, North Dakota, and South Dakota, all 1889; Wyoming and Idaho, 1890; Utah, 1896; Oklahoma, 1907; and New Mexico and Arizona, 1912. By 1912, as thousands had long hoped, the nation stretched west from the Atlantic to the Pacific and south from Canada to Mexico.

Bibliography

Bakker, Elna, and Richard G. Lillard. *The Great Southwest: The Story of a Land and Its People*. Palo Alto, CA: American West Publishing, 1972.

Bartlett, Richard A. *The New Country: A Social History of the American Frontier, 1776–1890*. New York: Oxford University Press, 1974.

Blake, Arthur, and Pamela Dailey. *The Gold Rush of 1849: Staking a Claim in California*. Brookfield, CT: Millbrook Press, 1995.

Brown, Dee. *The American West*. New York: Charles Scribner's Sons, 1994.

———. *The Westerners*. New York: Holt, Rinehart and Winston, 1974.

Carruth, Gorton. *The Encyclopedia of American Facts and Dates*, 9th Edition. New York: HarperCollins, 1993.

Coit, Margaret, and the Editors of *Life*. *The Sweep Westward* (Volume 4: 1829–1849, of the *Life* History of the United States). New York: Time, Inc., 1974.

Cooke, Alistair. *Alistair Cooke's America*. New York: Knopf, 1973.

Dary, David. *Seeking Pleasure in the Old West*. New York: Knopf, 1995.

Delgado, James P. *To California by Sea: A Maritime History of the California Gold Rush*. Columbia, SC: University of South Carolina Press, 1990.

Duffus, R. L. *The Santa Fe Trail*. London: Longmans, Green, 1930.

The Editors of Time-Life Books with text by Huston Horn. *The Old West: The Pioneers*. New York: Time-Life Books, 1974.

———. *The Old West: The Spanish West*. New York: Time-Life Books, 1976.

———. with text by Robert Wallace. *The Old West: The Miners*. New York: Time Inc., 1976.

———. with text by Joan Swallow Reiter. *The Old West: The Women*. Alexandria, VA: Time-Life Books, 1978.

Farrell, Cliff. *The Mighty Land*. Garden City, NY: Doubleday, 1975.

Franzwa, Gregory M. *The Oregon Trail Revisited*. Tucson, AZ: Patrice Press, 1972.

Herb, Angela M. *Beyond the Mississippi: Early Expansion of the United States*. New York: Dutton, 1996.

Hill, William E. *The Oregon Trail: Yesterday and Today*. Caldwell, ID: Caxton Printers, 1994.

Howard, Robert West. *The South Pass Story*. New York: G. P. Putnam's Sons, 1968.

Levy, Joann. *They Saw the Elephant: Women in the California Gold Rush*. Hamden, CT: Shoe String Press, 1990.

Mattes, Merrill J. *The Great Platte River Road*. Lincoln, NE: University of Nebraska Press, 1987.

McGlashan, Charles Fayette. *History of the Donner Party: A Tragedy of the Sierra*. Stanford, CA: Stanford University Press, 1968.

Milner II, Clyde A., Carol A. O'Connor, and Martha A. Sandweiss, eds. *The Oxford History of the American West*. New York: Oxford University Press, 1994.

Page, Elizabeth. *Wagons West: A Story of the Oregon Trail*. New York: Farrar & Rinehart, 1930.

Potter, David Morris, ed. *Trail to California: The Overland Journal of Vincent Geiger and Wakeman Bryarly*. New Haven, CT: Yale University Press, 1945.

Stefoff, Rebecca. *The Oregon Trail in American History*. Springfield, NJ: Enslow, 1997.

———. *Children of the Westward Trail*. Brookfield, CT: Millbrook Press, 1996.

Stewart, George R. *Ordeal by Hunger: The Story of the Donner Party*. Lincoln, NE: University of Nebraska Press, 1986.

Unruh, John. *The Plains Across: The Overland Emigrants and the Trans-Mississippi West, 1840–60*. Chicago: University of Illinois Press, 1979.

Ward, Geoffrey C. *The West: An Illustrated History* (based on a documentary film script by Ward and Dayton Duncan). Boston: Little Brown, 1996.

Ware, Joseph E. *The Emigrant's Guide to California* (reprinted from the 1849 edition, with introduction and notes by John Caughey) New York: Da Capo Press, 1972.

Werner, Emmy E. *Pioneer Children on the Journey West*. Boulder, CO: Westview Press, 1995.

Wyman, Walker D., ed. *California Emigrant Letters: The Forty-Niners Write Home*. New York: Bookman, 1952.

Further Reading

The following list is made of books that should prove of special interest and value to young readers. They were all used in the preparation of this book.

Adams, Samuel Hopkins. *The Santa Fe Trail*. New York: Random House, 1951.

Barry, Erick. *When Wagons Rolled to Santa Fe*. Champaign, IL: Garrad, 1966.

Blake, Arthur, and Pamela Dailey. *The Gold Rush of 1849: Staking a Claim in California*. Brookfield, CT: Millbrook Press, 1995.

Calvert, Patricia. *Great Lives: The American Frontier*. New York: Atheneum Books for Young Readers, 1997. (For chapter on Marcus and Narcissa Whitman.)

Dorian, Edith, and N. W. Wilson. *Trails West and the Men Who Made Them*. New York: Whittlesey House (McGraw-Hill), 1955.

Eggenhofer, Nick. *Wagons, Mules and Men: How the Frontier Moved West*. New York: Hastings House, 1961.

Erickson, Paul. *Daily Life in a Covered Wagon*. Washington, DC: Preservation Press, 1994.

Grant, Bruce. *Famous American Trails*. Chicago: Rand McNally, 1971.

Lavender, David. *The Trail to Santa Fe*. Boston: Houghton Mifflin, 1958.

Lyngheim, Linda. *Gold Rush Adventure*. Van Nuys, CA: Langtry Publications, 1988.

McNeese, Tim. *Western Wagon Trains*. New York: Crestwood House, 1993.

Monaghan, Jay, Editor-In-Chief. *The Book of the American West*. New York: Julian Messner, 1963.

Murphy, Virginia Reed. *Across the Plains in the Donner Party: A Personal Narrative of the Overland Trip to California, 1846–47*. Golden, CO: Outlook, 1980.

Stefoff, Rebecca. *The Oregon Trail in American History*. Springfield, NJ: Enslow, 1997.

———. *Children of the Westward Trail*. Brookfield, CT: Millbrook Press, 1996.

Young, Bob, and Jan Young. *The 49ers: The Story of the California Gold Rush*. New York: Julian Messner, 1966.

Index